Know Your Rights

A Citizen's Guide to the 4th, 5th, 6th, and 14th Amendments

This publication is for educational purposes only and is not legal advice.

Know Your Rights

A Citizen's Guide to the 4th, 5th, 6th, and 14th Amendments

This book is provided **for educational and informational purposes only**. It is **not legal advice** and does not create an attorney-client relationship. Laws vary by jurisdiction and individual circumstances, and the information contained in this publication may not apply to every situation. Readers are strongly encouraged to consult a licensed attorney or qualified legal professional for advice regarding their specific legal matters.

The author is not an attorney. The author holds a Certificate in Paralegal Studies and writes from professional experience in public service, compliance, and community education. Any errors or omissions are the responsibility of the author alone.

The information in this book reflects the law as of the date of publication. Legal standards and court decisions may change over time.

First Edition

Printed in the United States of America

Important Legal Disclaimer

This book is provided **for educational and informational purposes only**. It is **not legal advice**, and it does not create an attorney-client relationship. Laws vary by state and by individual circumstances, and the information in this guide may not apply to every situation.

If you are facing a legal issue, have been arrested, or are under investigation, you should seek advice from a **qualified attorney or legal professional** licensed in your jurisdiction. Do not rely solely on this book to make legal decisions about your specific case.

CONTENTS

Dedication

This book is dedicated to all Law Enforcement Officers, First Responders, and members of our military who serve with honor, courage, and dignity to protect our communities and our nation each day, as well as the healthcare professionals who care for others in times of crisis, and bus drivers, truck drivers, taxi drivers, airline pilots, and flight attendants who keep our country moving, and every day people who work hard to keep this country great.

This dedication extends to our state and local government workers and public officials who serve the public, often without recognition, as well as to everyday hard working-class people—from the wealthy to the average men and women in the street. Each plays a role in the strength and stability of our society.

This book is dedicated to you because the Constitution belongs to all of us, including all citizens and legal residents of the United States. It protects every person equally, regardless of title, profession, or status. The Constitution matters because it unites us under the rule of law, safeguards our freedoms, and reminds us that service, dignity, and justice are shared responsibilities in a free society.

*"**We the People of the United States**, in Order to form a more perfect Union, establish Justice, insure domestic Tranquility, provide for the common defense, promote the general Welfare, and secure the Blessings of Liberty to ourselves and our Posterity, do ordain and establish this Constitution for the United States of America."*

— Preamble to the United States Constitution

Acknowledgment

This book would not exist without the principles set forth in the United States Constitution and the generations of Americans who have worked to uphold it. The framers created a system rooted in liberty, accountability, and the rule of law—one that continues to guide and protect our nation centuries later.

I acknowledge the courts, judges, and legal professionals who interpret and apply constitutional principles every day. Through their decisions, the Constitution remains a living document, capable of responding to new challenges while preserving fundamental rights.

I also thank the educators, mentors, and community leaders who teach civics, history, and constitutional law—often without recognition. Their commitment ensures that knowledge is passed on and that future generations understand both their rights and responsibilities.

Most importantly, I acknowledge the everyday people who live under the Constitution protection: workers, students, parents, public servants, and citizens from all walks of life. This book is for those who believe that knowledge matters, that rights matter, and that an informed public is essential to a free society.

Finally, I thank you, the reader, for taking the time to learn, reflect, and engage. The Constitution only works when people understand it and insist that it be honored.

About the Author

Gideon A. Dunkley Jr., MBA, is a lifelong public servant, finance professional, and constitutional educator whose career reflects a deep commitment to accountability, service, and the rule of law. He graduated from Hyde Park High School in 1972 and began his higher education at Northeastern University, where he majored in Political Science. After two semesters at Northeastern University, he relocated from Boston to New York, continuing his academic and professional journey.

Mr. Dunkley earned a Bachelor of Science Degree in Accounting from CUNY Lehman College and later obtained a Paralegal Certificate from Bronx Community College, strengthening his understanding of law, due process, and civic rights. He also holds a Master of Business Administration with a concentration in Health Care Management.

From 1993 to 2015, Mr. Dunkley served for 22 years as a New York City Auxiliary Police Officer in the NYPD's 47th Precinct in the Bronx, supporting community safety and public trust by utilizing Courtesy, Respect and Professionalism towards his community in the 47th Precinct. Professionally, he has worked as an accountant and auditor for both the City and State of New York and is currently employed as a Financial Analyst at Weill Cornell Medicine in the Department of Medicine, Division of Infectious Diseases.

His diverse background in law enforcement, finance, and public service informs his passion for educating citizens about their constitutional rights and responsibilities because ignorance of the law is no excuse.

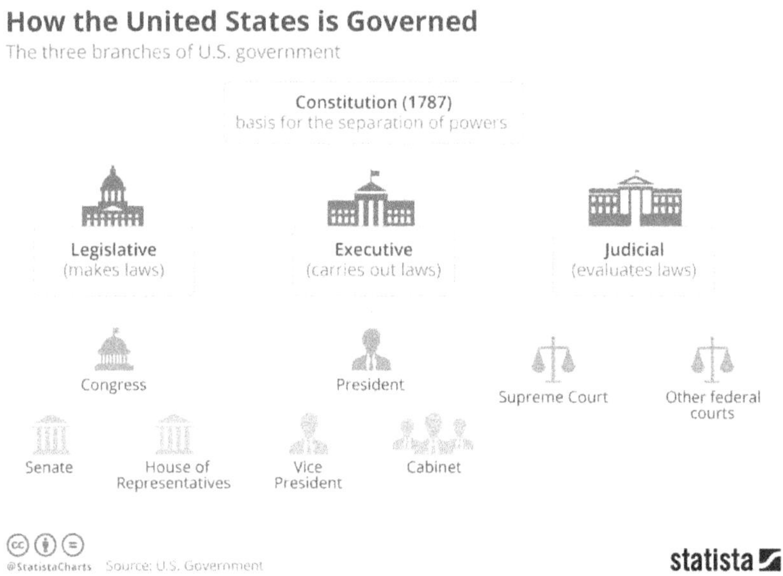

https://constitution.congress.gov

Foreword

I am not a lawyer, and I do not claim to be one. I write this guide as a trained paralegal and longtime public servant who has spent years working alongside attorneys, law enforcement professionals, and community organizations. Through that experience, I have seen how quickly an ordinary interaction with police can turn into a life-altering event, often because someone did not understand their basic constitutional rights.

I hold a Certificate in Paralegal Studies from CUNY Bronx Community College, and my professional background has placed me close to the legal system for decades. I have also served my community as an Auxiliary Police Officer, giving me a unique perspective on both sides of police encounters.

What I have learned is simple but important: Most Americans don't know their rights and most people do not get into trouble because they intend to break the law. They get into trouble because they speak when silence would protect them, consent when they have the right to refuse, or do not realize they can ask for legal counsel. This guide exists to address that gap in knowledge.

The Constitution belongs to everyone, not just lawyers and judges. The Fourth, Fifth, Sixth, and Fourteenth Amendments were written to protect ordinary people during moments of stress and imbalance of power. This book is meant to help readers understand those protections in plain language, without fear or intimidation.

The chapters that follow are not about disrespecting law enforcement or avoiding accountability. They are about understanding your rights so you can exercise them calmly and responsibly. When people know their rights, encounters are safer, fairer, and more just for everyone involved.

Introduction

The United States Constitution is the foundation of the American legal and political system because it establishes how the government is formed, how power is divided, and how individual rights are protected.

Written in 1787, the Constitution replaced the weak Articles of Confederation and created a stronger federal government without giving it unlimited power. It set clear rules for governance and made **the Constitution the highest law of the land,** meaning all laws and government actions must follow it.

A central feature of the Constitution is the creation of three separate branches of government: the legislative, executive, and judicial branches. Congress, the legislative branch, makes the laws; the President and executive agencies enforce the laws; and the courts, led by the Supreme Court, interpret the laws. This separation of powers prevents any one branch from gaining too much control. Each branch has checks on the others, such as presidential vetoes, congressional oversight, and judicial review, ensuring balance and accountability within the system.

The Constitution also matters because it protects the rights of the people from government abuse. The Bill of Rights guarantees freedoms such as speech, religion, due process, and **protection from unreasonable searches and seizures**. These rights apply to all levels of government and are enforced by the courts. Because the Constitution limits government power**, it ensures that citizens are**

governed by laws, not by the personal wishes of those in authority.

All government officials and members of the military must swear an oath to support and defend the Constitution because their duty is to the rule of law, not to any individual or political party. This oath reinforces the idea that no one is above the Constitution and that public power must be exercised within constitutional limits. The Constitution remains relevant today because it balances stability with flexibility, allowing change through amendments while **preserving the core principles of liberty, equality, and justice.**

The Constitution belongs to everyone. Learning your rights helps protect your future and the freedoms of others. Knowledge is protection. According to the United States Senate: The Constitution's first three words are ***"We the People"*** affirm that the government of the United States exist to serve its citizens.

16 Am Jur 2d, Sec 177 late 2d, Sec 256: *The general misconception is that any statute passed by legislators bearing the appearance of law constitutes the law of the land.* **The U.S. Constitution is the Supreme Law of the Land**, *and any statute, to be valid, must be in agreement.*

Marbury v. Madison (1803): *Arguably the most influential case in U.S. Supreme Court history. It established the principle of* **judicial review** *– an important addition to the system of checks and balances. It prevents any one branch of the government from becoming too powerful, Chief Justice John Marshal ruled* **"a law repugnant to the Constitution is void"** *- the power of federal courts to declare legislative and executive acts unconstitutional.*

Chapter 1
The Constitution on the Street

The Constitution is not just a historical document, or something discussed in courtrooms. It is a living set of rules that applies during everyday interactions between people and government officials, especially police officers. The Fourth, Fifth, Sixth, and Fourteenth Amendments shape what officers may do and what rights citizens retain during stops, searches, questioning, and arrests. These protections exist to balance government power with individual liberty.

An important concept that supports all of these constitutional protections is **jurisdiction**. In law, jurisdiction means legal authority, the power of a government body, court, or officer to act. Police officers, courts, and agencies are only allowed to exercise power within the limits of their lawful authority. When officials act outside their jurisdiction, their actions may be challenged and, in some cases, declared invalid.

Jurisdiction matters because different officials have different powers. Local police generally have authority only within certain geographic boundaries. Courts must have jurisdiction over both the type of case and the people involved before they can issue valid orders or warrants. Federal agencies operate under separate legal authority, and immigration enforcement is governed primarily by civil law rather than criminal law. Understanding these distinctions helps explain why not every badge carries the same power.

Jurisdiction is especially important when it comes to warrants. A valid warrant must be issued by a court with proper jurisdiction and must clearly state who is authorized to act and where. If a court lacks authority, the warrant may be invalid. This is why citizens are encouraged to calmly ask to see a warrant and check who issued it during certain encounters, particularly at homes or workplaces.

From a practical standpoint, citizens are not required to argue jurisdiction on the street. However, knowing that government power has limits explains why questions such as "Am I being detained?", Or "Am I free to go?" are so important. These questions help clarify whether an officer is acting within lawful authority.

The hook is simple yet powerful: because constitutional rights only have meaning when government power has boundaries, and jurisdiction is one of the most important boundaries the law provides.

Chapter 2
Traffic Stops and the Fourth Amendment

Traffic stops are the most common way people encounter police, and they are also one of the most legally significant. When an officer activates emergency lights and pulls a vehicle over, that driver and all passengers are considered seized under the Fourth Amendment. This seizure must be justified by reasonable suspicion that a traffic law was violated. The Supreme Court made this clear in *Delaware v. Prouse* (1979), holding that random or arbitrary traffic stops are unconstitutional.

Once a stop is lawfully initiated, police may request a driver's license, registration, and proof of insurance. These requests are permitted. However, what often follows goes beyond what the Constitution allows. Officers may ask where are you coming from, where are you going, or whether you have anything illegal in the car. You are not required to answer these questions. In *Rodriguez v. United States* (2015), the Court ruled that officers cannot extend a traffic stop beyond its original purpose unless new reasonable suspicion develops.

Searches and use of force during traffic stops are closely scrutinized under the Fourth Amendment. Just as important, courts strictly limit how long a traffic stop may last. In *Rodriguez v. United States* (2015), the Supreme Court ruled that police may not extend a traffic stop beyond the time reasonably required to address the original reason for the stop, such as writing a ticket or checking a driver's license, unless new reasonable suspicion of criminal activity develops. The

Court rejected the idea that officers may add even a brief delay for unrelated investigations, such as a K-9 dog sniff, without additional justification.

The Court explained that a traffic stop is lawful only for the duration of its mission. Once that mission is completed, the officer's authority ends. Any extension, no matter how short, becomes an unconstitutional seizure if it is unrelated to the original violation and unsupported by new suspicion. This ruling makes clear that convenience for law enforcement does not override constitutional limits.

Searches and use of force during traffic stops are also closely scrutinized under the Fourth Amendment. In *Barnes v. Felix* (2025), the Supreme Court addressed how courts must evaluate police use of force during a traffic stop. The case arose after Officer Roberto Felix fatally shot Ashtian Barnes during a stop for toll violations. Lower courts focused only on the final moments before the shooting, applying a narrow "moment-of-threat" analysis and granting the officer immunity.

From a practical standpoint, *Barnes v. Felix* reinforces an important point for citizens: traffic stops are not isolated moments frozen in time. Everything that happens, from how the stop begins to how it escalates, matters legally. For drivers, the safest approach remains consistent. Keep your hands visible. Be polite. Do not argue on the roadside. Provide required documents and limit your speech. If asked for consent to search, say clearly, "I do not consent to any searches."

The hook is one every defense attorney knows well: traffic stops are judged as a whole, and the fewer words you speak and the fewer risks you take, the less opportunity there is for a routine stop to turn into a constitutional crisis.

Chapter 3
Searches, Consent, and Plain View

Searches are where many police encounter cross from lawful to unconstitutional. The Fourth Amendment draws a firm line between what officers may observe and what they may search. Police do not need permission to look at what is openly visible, but they generally need a warrant, probable cause, or valid consent to go further. In real life, however, most unlawful searches occur not because police have a warrant, but because consent is given under pressure or confusion.

Consent is powerful because it removes many constitutional protections. In *Schneckloth v. Bustamonte* (1973), the Supreme Court ruled that consent must be voluntary, but officers are not required to tell you that you have the right to refuse. As a result, many people agree to searches simply because they feel intimidated or believe refusal will make matters worse. Courts later examine whether consent was voluntary, but by then the damage is often done.

The plain view doctrine allows officers to seize evidence without a warrant if three conditions are met: the officer must be lawfully present, the item must be in plain sight, and its criminal nature must be immediately obvious. In *Horton v. California* (1990), the Court clarified that plain view does not allow officers to search further or manipulate objects. In *Arizona v. Hicks* (1987), evidence was suppressed because an officer moved property to investigate, turning observation into an unlawful search.

Closely tied to illegal searches is the fruit of the poisonous tree doctrine. This rule means that when police obtain evidence through an unconstitutional search or seizure, not only is that evidence excluded, but anything discovered as a result of it may also be excluded. The Supreme Court laid the foundation for this principle in *Silverthorne Lumber Co. v. United States* (1920), expanded it in *Nardone v. United States* (1939), and firmly applied it in *Wong Sun v. United States* (1963). In simple terms, if the search is illegal, the evidence, and anything that flows from it, is usually unusable in court.

From a practical standpoint, this doctrine reinforces why refusing consent matters. An unlawful search can unravel an entire case, but only if the violation is preserved. Do not help create evidence. Do not open containers. Do not explain what officers might find. Say clearly, "I do not consent to any searches," and then remain silent.

The hook is one defense attorneys rely on constantly: when the tree is poisoned, the fruit cannot be used, but only if the violation happens in the first place.

Chapter 4
Stop and Frisk, Reasonable Suspicion, and Street Encounters

Stop-and-frisk encounters are among the most controversial uses of police power, and they are also among the most misunderstood. Under the Fourth Amendment, police may briefly stop a person if they have reasonable suspicion that criminal activity is taking place. This standard, established in *Terry v. Ohio* (1968), is lower than probable cause but higher than a hunch. Officers must be able to point to specific, articulable facts that justify the stop.

In New York, stop-and-frisk encounters are also governed by a state-specific framework established in *People v. De Bour* (1976). In that case, the New York Court of Appeals created a **four-level framework** that defines what police may do as an encounter escalates and what level of justification is required at each stage.

Under **Level One**, police may approach an individual and request information if they have an objective, credible reason to do so. This level does not allow detention and does not require suspicion of criminal activity. Under **Level Two**, known as the common-law right of inquiry, police must have founded suspicion that criminal activity is afoot. Officers may ask more pointed questions and may briefly detain a person, but they may not frisk without additional justification.

A frisk is even more limited. Under **Level Three**, police may conduct a pat-down of outer clothing for weapons only if they reasonably believe the person is armed and dangerous. A frisk is not a full search and may not be used to look for drugs, evidence, or identification. Courts have consistently ruled that when officers exceed this narrow scope, any evidence discovered may be suppressed.

Under **Level Four**, police must have probable cause, which permits a full arrest and a search incident to that arrest. Skipping levels or escalating an encounter without meeting the required legal standard violates constitutional protections and may result in evidence being excluded.

The Fourteenth Amendment plays a critical role in stop-and-frisk cases. It guarantees equal protection under the law and requires that policing practices be applied fairly and without discrimination. Courts have examined patterns of stops to determine whether enforcement practices unfairly target specific communities. While these claims are often difficult to prove, documentation and consistency matter greatly.

From a practical perspective, the safest response during a stop-and-frisk encounter is to remain calm and non-confrontational. Do not run. Do not physically resist. Ask calmly, "Am I being detained? Am I free to go?" If you are detained, you may invoke your right to remain silent. Pay close attention to details such as time, location, and officer behavior, as these facts may later become important.

The hook is one New York courts repeatedly return to: police authority increases only when legal justification increases, and constitutional protections weaken only when the law permits it.

Chapter 5
The Fifth Amendment and the Right to Remain Silent

The Fifth Amendment is often summarized in one familiar phrase: the right to remain silent. In practice, it is one of the most powerful protections a citizen has during a police encounter. The amendment exists to prevent the government from forcing people to help convict themselves. Yet many cases unravel not because of physical evidence, but because of words spoken under pressure.

The Supreme Court's decision in *Miranda v. Arizona* (1966) requires police to advise individuals of their rights before custodial interrogation. However, Miranda warnings do not apply in every interaction. Officers may ask questions before arrest, during traffic stops, or in casual conversations. In *Berghuis v. Thompkins* (2010), the Court ruled that simply staying quiet is not enough. A person must clearly invoke the right to remain silent.

This distinction matters. Saying nothing may feel safe, but courts have allowed questioning to continue unless the right is verbally asserted. The safest approach is to say, "I am invoking my Fifth Amendment right to remain silent." Once this statement is made, questioning must stop. Police may continue routine booking questions, but they cannot interrogate you about alleged crimes.

From a practical standpoint, silence is not rude or suspicious. It is a constitutional choice. Police are trained to gather information, and they may appear friendly or concerned. They may suggest that cooperation will help you. Experience shows that explanations often create inconsistencies that later appear damaging in court.

The hook is one that defense attorneys repeat often: no statement is better than a bad statement, and silence cannot be misquoted.

Chapter 6
Questioning Without Arrest and Voluntary Encounters

Not every police encounter involves handcuffs or an arrest. Officers frequently engage people in what the law calls voluntary or consensual encounters. During these interactions, police may ask questions without having reasonable suspicion or probable cause. The key legal issue is whether a reasonable person would feel free to leave.

In *Florida v. Bostick* (1991), the Supreme Court held that a police encounter is voluntary if a person feels free to decline requests or terminate the interaction. However, the reality of police authority can make this distinction unclear. Uniforms, weapons, and tone of voice can create pressure even when officers say you are not detained.

The most important question you can ask during any encounter is simple: "Am I free to leave?" If the answer is yes, you may walk away calmly. If the answer is no, the encounter has become a detention, and Fourth Amendment protections apply. At that point, you may invoke your Fifth Amendment right to remain silent, and request to speak to a lawyer.

From a defense perspective, voluntary questioning is risky because it creates statements without the safeguards that exist after arrest. Officers may take notes or record conversations. These statements are often introduced in court as admissions.

The practical advice is consistent and effective. Do not guess. Do not speculate. Do not try to talk your way out of suspicion. Ask if you are free to go. If not, assert your rights clearly.

The hook is one that surprises many clients: most damaging statements are made when people believe they are helping themselves.

Chapter 7
Arrests, Charges, and the Sixth Amendment Right to Counsel

An arrest marks a turning point in any police encounter. Once a person is arrested and formally charged, the Sixth Amendment becomes central to everything that follows. This amendment guarantees the right to assistance of counsel, meaning the government may not prosecute someone without allowing access to a lawyer. The Supreme Court made this protection clear in *Gideon v. Wainwright* (1963), holding that states must provide an attorney to defendants who cannot afford one.

The right to counsel attaches once adversarial judicial proceedings begin, such as a formal charge, arraignment, or indictment. At that point, police and prosecutors may not deliberately elicit statements from you without your lawyer present. Courts have repeatedly emphasized that this right exists to level an uneven playing field. The government has investigators, legal training, and resources. The accused has the right to professional guidance, not guesswork.

In real life, many people waive this right without realizing it. Police may continue to ask questions after arrest, hoping for cooperation. They may suggest that asking for a lawyer will make things worse or delay release. These suggestions are misleading. Invoking your right to counsel is not an admission of guilt. It is a constitutional safeguard.

From a practical standpoint, the rule is simple: once arrested, say clearly, "I want a lawyer." Say nothing else. Do not discuss the case with officers, cellmates, or over jail phones, which are often recorded. Even casual comments can be used in court.

The hook is one every defense attorney understands: the sooner a lawyer enters the case, the fewer mistakes there are to fix later.

Chapter 8
The Fourteenth Amendment and Equal Protection

The Fourteenth Amendment ensures that constitutional rights apply equally to everyone and that states may not deprive any person of life, liberty, or property without due process of law. It is the amendment that brings the protections of the Fourth, Fifth, and Sixth Amendments into state courts, where most criminal cases are decided. Without it, constitutional rights would vary from state to state.

Equal protection is a core principle of the Fourteenth Amendment. It requires that laws be enforced fairly and without discrimination. Courts have recognized that selective enforcement based on race, ethnicity, or other improper factors undermines public trust and violates constitutional guarantees. While proving discriminatory intent is difficult, courts do consider patterns, data, and credible testimony.

The Fourteenth Amendment also guarantees due process, which means fairness in legal procedures. This includes timely hearings, notice of charges, and meaningful opportunities to challenge evidence. When police violate constitutional rules, courts may exclude evidence or dismiss charges altogether.

From a practical perspective, documentation matters. Write down what happened as soon as possible. Note times, locations, and officer behavior. Save videos and witness information. These details can later support constitutional claims.

The hook is one that resonates beyond any single case: constitutional rights have meaning only when they are enforced equally and consistently.

Chapter 9
Federal Agents and Your Constitutional Rights

Encounters with federal agents often feel more intimidating than interactions with local police, but the Constitution does not change simply because the badge does. FBI agents, ICE officers, and other federal law enforcement officials are bound by the same Fourth, Fifth, Sixth, and Fourteenth Amendments. The authority they carry is significant, but it is not unlimited. Understanding this difference is critical, especially for immigrants and mixed-status families.

The Fourth Amendment applies fully to federal agents. They may not enter your home without a valid judicial warrant signed by a judge, unless you consent or an emergency exists. Many people are shown administrative warrants, particularly in immigration enforcement. These documents do not authorize entry into a private residence. Courts have consistently held that consent obtained through confusion or intimidation is not valid consent.

The Fifth Amendment right to remain silent applies equally in federal encounters. You are not required to answer questions about your immigration status, your place of birth, or your travel history. In fact, statements made to federal agents often carry serious consequences. Never speak to a federal agent without a lawyer. If you lie to a federal agent, it's a felony. Federal cases rely heavily on recorded interviews and written statements. Silence, when properly invoked, is your strongest protection.

From a practical standpoint, the safest response to federal questioning is calm firmness. Ask to see a warrant and then read it carefully. Do not open the door unless you are legally required to do so. If you can, try to install a doorbell camera so you can see and record who is at your front door. Say clearly, "I choose to remain silent, and I want to speak to a lawyer." Do not sign documents without legal advice.

Judicial Warrants: A judicial warrant is issued by a judge or magistrate after a finding of probable cause. It authorizes law enforcement officers to take specific actions, such as entering a home, conducting a search, or making an arrest. Judicial warrants must identify the court that issued them, the person or place involved, and the scope of authority granted. When properly issued, a judicial warrant may lawfully compel compliance.

Administrative Warrants: An administrative warrant is issued by a government agency rather than a judge. These warrants are commonly used in civil enforcement matters, including immigration proceedings. Administrative warrants do not require a judicial finding of probable cause and generally do not authorize entry into a private home without consent. They may allow agents to take certain administrative actions, but their legal power is more limited than that of a judicial warrant.

Why the Difference Matters: Understanding the difference between judicial and administrative warrants is critical because the level of authority is not the same. A judicial warrant carries the power of the court, while an administrative warrant reflects agency authority only. Confusing the two can lead people to believe they must comply when the law does not require it. Knowing the distinction helps individuals protect their homes, assert their rights calmly, and avoid unintentionally giving consent where none is required.

The hook is one that federal courts reinforce repeatedly: federal authority may be powerful, but constitutional rights do not shrink in its presence.

Chapter 10
Winning Your Case Before Court Begins

Most criminal cases are not decided by juries. They are shaped long before trial, often during the very first encounter between a citizen and law enforcement. The Constitution is most effective when it is exercised early, calmly, and consistently. Defense attorneys know that the strongest cases often begin with clients who understood their rights from the start.

Every chapter in this book points to the same core lesson: police encounters create evidence. That evidence can come from searches, statements, or behavior. The Fourth Amendment controls what police may take. The Fifth Amendment controls what you may say. The Sixth Amendment ensures professional guidance once charges are filed. The Fourteenth Amendment demands fairness in how all of this is applied.

Practical habits make a difference. Stay calm. Do not argue on the street. Ask clear questions. Invoke your rights respectfully. Document what happens as soon as possible. These steps do not guarantee dismissal, but they significantly improve your position in court.

Courts examine credibility, consistency, and legality. Judges do not expect perfection, but they do expect law enforcement to follow constitutional rules. When those rules are violated, remedies exist including suppression of evidence and dismissal of charges.

The final hook is one worth remembering: the smartest legal victories often come from the moments when a person chooses not to speak, not to consent, and not to surrender rights they never had to give away.

Appendix A
Plain-Language Summary of Key Constitutional Amendments

This appendix provides a brief, easy-to-understand summary of the First, Fourth, Fifth, Sixth, and Fourteenth Amendments discussed throughout this guide. These amendments work together to protect citizens during encounters with law enforcement and within the criminal justice system.

The First Amendment – Freedom of Expression and Assembly

The First Amendment protects fundamental freedoms essential to a democratic society, including: freedom of speech, freedom of the press, freedom of religion, freedom of peaceful assembly, and the right to petition the government.

In everyday life, this amendment protects the right to verbally question or criticize government actions, to peacefully protest, and to record police activity in public spaces, as long as those activities do not interfere with lawful duties. These protections allow citizens to express themselves, seek accountability, and participate in civic life without fear of government retaliation.

The Fourth Amendment – Protection Against Unreasonable Searches and Seizures

The Fourth Amendment protects people from unreasonable searches and seizures by the government. In simple terms, police generally must have a lawful reason to stop you and a lawful reason to search you.

In most cases, this means they need a warrant issued by a judge based on probable cause. There are limited exceptions, such as emergencies or certain vehicle searches, but the rule is that your person, home, and belongings are protected.

This amendment exists to prevent arbitrary or abusive government intrusion. If police violate the Fourth Amendment, courts may exclude the evidence they obtained. This is why refusing consent to searches and asking whether you are free to leave are powerful and lawful actions.

The Fifth Amendment – The Right Against Self-Incrimination

The Fifth Amendment protects your right not to incriminate yourself. This is commonly known as the right to remain silent. You cannot be forced to answer questions that may be used against you in a criminal case. This amendment also guarantees that the government must follow fair procedures before depriving someone of liberty.

In practice, this means you may refuse to answer questions from police and you may ask for a lawyer. To fully protect this right, you must clearly state that you are invoking it. Silence alone may not be enough.

The Fifth Amendment exists because words spoken under pressure are often unreliable and unfairly used.

The Sixth Amendment – The Right to Counsel and a Fair Trial

The Sixth Amendment guarantees the right to a lawyer once criminal charges are filed. If you cannot afford an attorney, the court must provide one. This amendment also protects your right to a speedy and public trial, an impartial jury, and the ability to confront witnesses against you.

The purpose of the Sixth Amendment is to ensure fairness. Criminal law is complex, and no person should have to face the power of the government alone. Asking for a lawyer is not an admission of guilt - it is a constitutional right.

The Eighth Amendment - Ratified in 1791 as part of the Bill of Rights, prohibits the federal government from imposing excessive bail, excessive fines, or cruel and unusual punishments. It serves to limit the severity of penalties, covering areas such as the death penalty, prison conditions, and bail amounts.

The Fourteenth Amendment – Due Process and Equal Protection

The Fourteenth Amendment makes the protections of the Bill of Rights apply to the states where most criminal cases occur. It guarantees due process, meaning fairness in legal procedures, and equal protection, meaning laws must be enforced fairly and without discrimination.

This amendment is critical because it ensures that constitutional rights do not depend on where you live or who you are. It also allows courts to address discriminatory policing and unfair legal practices. Without the Fourteenth Amendment, many of the rights discussed in this guide would not be enforceable in state courts.

Search & Consent Quick Guide

This quick guide is designed to be a sample of simple, easy-to-remember reference for everyday encounters with law enforcement. It summarizes your core rights related to searches and consent under the Fourth and 5th Amendments. Please note, this is for educational purposes only and is not legal advice.

The Golden Rule

Police generally need **a judicial warrant, probable cause, or your consent** to search you, your vehicle, or your home. If you do not give consent, they must rely on the law, not pressure.

What Police Officers CAN Do:

During a traffic stop, they can run your license plate to determine the registered owner of the vehicle and ask questions during a traffic stop or encounter. They may ask you several questions: Do you know why I stopped you? Where are you coming from? Where are you going? Do you mind if I search your vehicle?

They can request your license, registration, and insurance during a traffic stop. But you do not have to answer any questions once you plead the 5th. You can say politely, "No, Officer. I do not know why you stopped me." let the officer explain why you were stopped. Then you can politely say, "Officer, I am exercising my right to remain silent." alternatively you can just say you are pleading the 5th. and stop talking. Do not engage in small or petty talk because a traffic stop is an investigation - anything you say can be used against you in a court of law. Plead the 5th, DO NOT CONSENT TO ANY SEARCHES, and stay quiet. They may ask you if you have any weapons or contraband in the vehicle. You may respond by saying "Officer I wish to remain silent, and I want to speak to my attorney." At the end of a vehicle stop, you want to arrive at your destination alive, not in handcuffs and not in jail. They cannot stop you from exercising your constitutional rights. *Berkemer v. McCarty* - 468 U.S. 420 (1984), and *Shuttlesworth v. City of Birmingham*, Alabama, 373 U.S, 262 (1963). Every vehicle stop is a 4th Amendment seizure. Always Plead the 5th, say it, and stop talking and ask for an attorney if necessary. 6th Amendment, *Gideon v. Wainwright* (1963).

The officer can look at anything that is in plain view while lawfully present.

The officer can ask for your consent to search your vehicle. **NEVER EVER CONSENT TO ANY SEARCHES and always plead the 5th and 6th if necessary.**

The police can trick you and lie to you: **to obtain your consent, to obtain your confession, and ultimately to obtain your conviction**. Always plead the 5th and NEVER CONSENT. Always request to speak to an attorney if you are being detained or arrested. They must read you your Miranda warning rights (*Miranda v. Arizona.* 1966). Request to speak to an attorney and then keep silent.

The first thing most police officers do during a vehicle stop is to run your license plate to ascertain who is the registered owner and whether or not any infraction is on either the vehicle or the registered owner. A car stop is an investigation for a vehicle or traffic violation but can escalate into an arrest. The police officer needs probable cause for detention and an arrest. Always invoke your 5th Amendment right to remain silent and say it, then remain silent and never CONSENT to any searches or anything else.

The police can order you out of your vehicle during a lawful traffic stop, *Pennsylvania v. Mimms* (1977). Please the 5th, and 6th if necessary.

What Police Officers CANNOT Lawfully Do Without Legal Justification or your CONSENT:

Search your person, car, phone, or home without a **judicial warrant**, **probable cause**, or voluntary **CONSENT**. Always INVOKE your 5TH Amendment right to remain silent, 6th Amendment if necessary and NEVER CONSENT.

They cannot extend the mission of a traffic stop beyond its original purpose without new reasonable suspicion (*Rodriguez v. United States*).

They cannot move or manipulate items to create plain view (*Arizona v. Hicks*).

They cannot use evidence obtained from an illegal search (*Mapp v. Ohio; Wong Sun v. United States*)

Officers generally cannot confiscate your phone, delete recordings, or demand you stop recording or filming them in public unless you are interfering with their duties. Always keep a safe distance.

What to say and Do during a Stop

You can use these words (this is for educational purposes only, this is not legal advice, always seek the advice of a lawyer, every situation is different):

- "I do not consent to any searches."
- "Am I being detained, or am I free to go?"
- "I am exercising my right to remain silent, plead the 5th."
- If you are free to go, leave quietly.
- If detained politely say, "What is the lawful reason for my detention? I wish to speak to a lawyer. I am exercising my right to remain silent."

- If asked to exit your vehicle you can ask if this is a command or a request. If it is a command, leave the vehicle and make sure the windows and doors are closed behind you. Keep your key(s) in your pocket or purse and ask politely what is the lawful reason for the command. Then say that you do not want to consent to any searches. You can also ask if you are being detained and why. If you are being detained, immediately ask to speak to an attorney and say that you wish to exercise your right to remain silent.
- You can record the police. The First Amendment rights generally protect the right to photograph or film police officers performing their duties in public spaces, as this acts as a form of free speech and press. This right is not absolute and is subject to "reasonable time, place, and manner restrictions". Recording cannot physically interfere with lawful police actions, such as arrests or investigations. Try to always keep a dash cam in your vehicle just in case you may need it to record an encounter and always keep a safe distance when recording.
- If you must appear in court, ask the prosecutor or judge if the law enforcement officer is on the Brady List.
- If you must sign for a ticket, print your name and then write / UCC 1-308, Without Prejudice, meaning - All Rights Reserved or V.C. or TDC. https://www.law.cornell.edu/ucc/1/1-308.

You do not need to explain or justify yourself. In *Shuttlesworth v. City of Birmingham, Alabama, 373 U.S, 262 (1963)* "There can be no sanction or penalty imposed upon one because of his exercise of Constitutional rights."

5. What NOT to Do

- Do not argue or physically resist. Stay quiet and calm.
- Do not joke, guess, or volunteer information.
- Do not engage in small talk. This is an investigation.
- Do not open containers, bags, or your trunk.
- Do not say "go ahead" or nod yes.
- Do not exit the vehicle unless it is a command to do so.
- If you must open the glove compartment for documents, tell the officer.
- Never drink and drive.
- Never resist.

6. Why Refusing Consent Matters

If a search is illegal, the evidence, and anything that flows from it, may be excluded under the fruit of the poisonous tree doctrine (*Silverthorne Lumber Co.; Wong Sun*). This protection only works if you DO NOT CONSENT.

7. Remember

Silence is not guilt. It is your 5th Amendment right, but you must say it. If necessary, you can invoke both your 5th and 6th Amendments rights. Consent can never be taken back.

Calm behavior protects your rights and your safety.

Bottom Line: You cannot stop police from asking, but you can stop them from searching by knowing and using your 4th Amendment rights, and you have the right to remain silent by invoking your 5th Amendment right, and NEVER EVER CONSENT to any searches.

Appendix B
Supreme Court and Federal Cases Cited in This Book

Below is a consolidated list of key court decisions referenced throughout this guide. These cases shape how constitutional rights are applied during police encounters, traffic stops, questioning, arrests, and court proceedings.

Fourth Amendment – Stops, Searches, and Use of Force

Every police stop is an investigation that comes under the 4th Amendment.

- *Mapp v. Ohio* (1961) – Illegally obtained evidence cannot be used in court.
- *Silverthorne Lumber Co. v. United States* (1920) – Evidence derived from illegal searches is inadmissible.
- *Nardone v. United States* (1939) – This case coined the phrase "fruit of the poisonous tree."
- *Wong Sun v. United States* (1963) – This case extended exclusion to evidence derived from unconstitutional searches or seizures.
- *Terry v. Ohio* (1968) – This case enables brief stop and frisk based only on reasonable suspicion.

- *Delaware v. Prouse* (1979) – Random traffic stops are unconstitutional.
- *Carroll v. United States* (1925) – Automobile exception
- *Schneckloth v. Bustamonte* (1973) – Consent must be voluntary.
- *Horton v. California* (1990) – Limits of plain view
- *Arizona v. Hicks* (1987) – Manipulating objects violates the Fourth Amendment.
- *Rodriguez v. United States* (2015) – No prolonging traffic stops without new suspicion.
- *Graham v. Connor* (1989) – Use of force is judged by totality of circumstances.
- *Barnes v. Felix* (2025) – Full context required for traffic-stop force analysis.
- *Pennsylvania v. Mimms (1977)* - The Supreme Court held that a police officer may order a driver out of a vehicle during a lawful traffic stop.
- *Maryland v. Wilson (1997)* - Police officers can order a passenger out of a vehicle during a lawfully stopped vehicle.
- *Brendlin v. California (2007)* – Established that a passenger in a vehicle stopped by police is "seized" under the Fourth Amendment, meaning they have the same right to challenge the legality of the stop.
- *Texas v. Brown, 460 U.S. 730 (1983)* - This case clarified the "plain view" doctrine, allowing police to seize evidence without a warrant if its incriminating nature is immediately apparent.

- *Morales v. Chadbourne (July 2015)* – First Circuit Court of Appeals ruled that ICE agents must have probable cause to issue immigration detainers, as such detentions constitute a seizure under the Fourth Amendment, and that state officials can be held liable for unlawful detention of U.S. citizens.

- *United States v. Brignoni-Ponce (1975)* is a landmark Supreme Court case that ruled Border Patrol agents on "roving patrols" cannot stop a vehicle near the border solely because the occupants appear to be of Mexican ancestry. The Court held that such stops violate the Fourth Amendment protection against unreasonable searches and seizures, stating that roving patrols must have reasonable suspicion - based on "specific articulable facts" - to stop a vehicle.
- *Payton v. New York* (1980) is a landmark United States Supreme Court case that established a critical protection for privacy under the **Fourth Amendment**. The Court ruled 6–3 that police may not enter a private residence to make a routine felony arrest without a warrant, except in cases of exigent circumstances (emergencies).
- *Riley v. California* (2014), the U.S. Supreme Court unanimously ruled that police generally must obtain a warrant to search the digital contents of a cell phone seized from an individual who has been arrested.

Fifth Amendment – Silence and Self -Incrimination

- *Miranda v. Arizona* (1966) - is a landmark U.S. Supreme Court case that established the requirement for law enforcement to inform suspects of their constitutional rights before custodial interrogation or detention. This case gives people the right to refuse to answer questions and also states that anything said can and will be used against the suspect in a court of law.

- *Berkemer v. McCarty (1984)* - McCarty, 468 U.S. 420 (1984), is a decision of the United States Supreme Court that ruled that a person in police custody following a misdemeanor traffic offense was entitled to the protections of the Fifth Amendment pursuant to the decision in *Miranda v. Arizona 384 U.S. 436 (1966).*

- *Berghuis v. Thompkins* (2010) - the U.S. Supreme Court ruled that a suspect must clearly and explicitly invoke their right to remain silent. The court held that simply staying silent during an interrogation is not enough to stop police questioning.

- *Salinas v. Texas (2013)* - is a landmark Supreme Court decision that established that the Fifth Amendment's privilege against self-incrimination does not protect a suspect's silence during a non-custodial police interview unless they expressly invoke that right.

- *United States v. Williams*, 504 U.S. 36 (1992), is a landmark Supreme Court case holding that federal courts do not have the supervisory power to require prosecutors to present "substantial exculpatory evidence" to a grand jury. Justice Antonin Scalia, writing for a 5-4 majority, emphasized that the grand jury is an institution separate from the courts, and its historical role is to assess whether there is an adequate basis for a criminal charge, not to determine guilt or innocence.

Sixth Amendment – Right to Counsel

- *Gideon v. Wainwright* (1963) – is a landmark U.S. Supreme Court case that established the constitutional right for indigent defendants to be provided legal counsel in state criminal trials. The Court unanimously ruled that the Sixth Amendment's guarantee of counsel is a fundamental right essential to a fair trial, made obligatory on the states via the Fourteenth Amendment's Due Process Clause. It also states that the accused has the right to consult with a lawyer and have one present during questioning.

Fourteenth Amendment – Due Process and Equal Protection

- *Florida v. Bostick* (1991) - is a landmark U.S. Supreme Court case that clarified the standards for seizures and consensual searches under the Fourth Amendment, specifically in the context of police sweeps on public transportation.

- *Brady v. Maryland* (1963) - The U.S. Supreme Court established that the prosecution's suppression of evidence favorable to an accused violates the Due Process Clause of the Fourteenth Amendment.

  This landmark ruling created the Brady Rule, which mandates that prosecutors must disclose all material exculpatory evidence to the defense—regardless of whether the withholding was intentional or in good faith. This created the Brady List.

  - *Brady List:* Law enforcement agencies now maintain *Brady Lists* of officers with known credibility issues (e.g., prior dishonesty) that must be disclosed to defense counsel in cases where they testify.

Appendix C
Plain-Language Case Summaries

Mapp v. Ohio (1961) – Illegally obtained evidence cannot be used in court.

Silverthorne Lumber Co. v. United States (1920) – Government cannot benefit from illegal searches.

Nardone v. United States (1939) – This introduced fruit of the poisonous tree doctrine.

Wong Sun v. United States (1963) – Extended exclusionary rule to derived evidence

Terry v. Ohio (1968) – Allows stop-and-frisk based on reasonable suspicion

People v. De Bour (1976) – New York four-level street encounter framework

Delaware v. Prouse (1979) – Random traffic stops are unconstitutional.

Carroll v. United States (1925) – Automobile exception to warrant requirement

Schneckloth v. Bustamonte (1973) – Consent searches must be voluntary.

Horton v. California (1990) – Plain-view doctrine limits

Arizona v. Hicks (1987) – Manipulating objects is a search

Rodriguez v. United States (2015) – Stops cannot be prolonged without suspicion.

Graham v. Connor (1989) – Objective reasonableness for police force

Barnes v. Felix (2025) – Full context required in force analysis

Miranda v. Arizona (1966) – Right to remain silent warnings required

Berghuis v. Thompkins (2010) – Silence must be clearly invoked.

Gideon v. Wainwright (1963) – Right to counsel is guaranteed.

Florida v. Bostick (1991) – Defines voluntary police encounters

Brady v. Maryland (1963) – Established the Brandy list for Law Enforcement Officers

Salinas v. Texas (2013) – You must expressly invoke your 5th Amendment right to remain silent.

Pennsylvania v. Mimms (1977) - is a landmark U.S. Supreme Court case that significantly expanded police authority during traffic stops. The Supreme Court held that a police officer may order a driver out of a vehicle during a lawful traffic stop.

Morales v. Chadbourne (July 2015) – First Circuit Court of Appeals ruled that ICE agents must have probable cause to issue immigration detainers, as such detentions constitute a seizure under the Fourth Amendment, and that state officials can be held liable for unlawful detention of U.S. citizens.

Payton v. New York (1980) is a landmark United States Supreme Court case that established a critical protection for privacy under the Fourth Amendment. The Court ruled 6–3 that police may not enter a private residence to make a routine felony arrest without a warrant, except in cases of **exigent circumstances** (emergencies).

United States v. Brignoni-Ponce (1975) is a landmark Supreme Court case that ruled Border Patrol agents on "roving patrols" cannot stop a vehicle near the border solely because the occupants appear to be of Mexican ancestry. The Court held that such stops violate the **Fourth Amendment** protection against unreasonable searches and seizures, stating that roving patrols must have **reasonable suspicion**—based on "specific articulable facts"—to stop a vehicle.

Additional information and other important cases:

Understanding UCC 1-308 / Without Prejudice

UCC 1-308, founded in the Uniform Commercial Code, protects a person's right to comply with a demand or contract without waiving their legal rights. It's a lawful way to perform, sign, or pay *under protest* while reserving the right to challenge the issue later.
https://www.law.cornell.edu/wex/ucc;
https://www.law.cornell.edu/ucc/1/1-308

Title 42 Section 1983, 1985, 1986 (Civil Rights):

Title 42 of the U.S. Code contains the primary federal statutes used to enforce constitutional and civil rights through civil litigation. Sections 1983, 1985, and 1986 originate from the Civil Rights Act of 1871 (also known as the Ku Klux Klan Act) and provide distinct legal mechanisms for holding individuals and entities accountable for rights violations.

Section 1983: Civil Action for Deprivation of Rights

This is the most frequently cited civil rights statute. It allows individuals to sue for violations of rights secured by the U.S. Constitution or federal laws.

- **Key Requirement:** The defendant must have acted *under color of law*, meaning they were using power granted by a state, local government, or territory.
- **Common Targets:** State and local officials, such as police officers (for excessive force or false arrest), prison guards, and school administrators.

- **Limitations:** It does not apply to federal officials (who are instead subject to Bivens actions) or to states themselves, as states are not considered "persons" under this statute.

Section 1985: Conspiracy to Interfere with Civil Rights

This section addresses situations where two or more persons conspire to deprive someone of their civil rights.

- **Scope:** It specifically prohibits conspiracies to prevent officers from performing duties, to obstruct justice (such as intimidating witnesses or jurors), or to deprive individuals of equal protection under the law.
- **Distinct Feature:** Unlike Section 1983, some parts of Section 1985 can apply to private individuals if they conspire together, even without a *under color of law* requirement, provided there is a class-based, discriminatory animus.

Section 1986: Action for Neglect to Prevent

This section creates a secondary form of liability for those who could have stopped a conspiracy mentioned in Section 1985.

- **Requirement:** A person must have knowledge that a Section 1985 conspiracy is about to occur, have the power to prevent or aid in preventing it, and neglect or refuse to do so.
- **Statute of Limitations:** Actions under Section 1986 must generally be commenced within one year after the cause of action accrued.

United States Code Title 18 section 241 and 242:

Sections 241 and 242 of Title 18 of the United States Code are the primary federal criminal statutes used by the Department of Justice to prosecute civil rights violations. While they share the goal of protecting constitutional rights, they differ in who can be charged and what constitutes the crime.

Section 241: Conspiracy Against Rights

This statute makes it a felony for two or more persons to agree to injure, threaten, or intimidate anyone in the free exercise of any right secured by the Constitution or U.S. laws.

- **Who it applies to:** Though it can apply to government officials, it focuses primarily on private individuals.
- **Key Requirement:** It requires a conspiracy (an agreement between two or more people). Unlike many other conspiracy laws, it does not require an overt act to be committed for a conviction.
- **Penalties:** These can be up to 10 years in prison. If death results, or if the act includes kidnapping or sexual abuse, it is punishable by up to life in prison or the death penalty.

Section 242: Deprivation of Rights Under Color of Law

This statute makes it a crime for a person acting under color of law to willfully deprive someone of their constitutional or federal rights.

- **Who it applies to:** This applies to government officials such as police officers, prison guards, and judges, who use their authority to violate a person's rights.
- **Key Requirement:** The defendant must have acted under actual or apparent legal authority (color of law). It also

requires specific intent, meaning the official must have willfully intended to deprive the victim of their rights.

- **Penalties:** A basic violation is a misdemeanor punishable by up to one year. If bodily injury or weapons are involved, it becomes a felony (up to 10 years). If death, kidnapping, or sexual abuse occurs, penalties can reach life imprisonment or the death penalty.

https://www.law.cornell.edu

28 U.S.C. § 1291 is the federal statute that grants United States courts of appeals jurisdiction over all final decisions of the district courts. https://www.law.cornell.edu/uscode/text/28/1291

42 U.S.C. § 1988, titled Proceedings in Vindication of Civil Rights, is a federal law that primarily allows courts to award attorney's fees to the winning party in civil rights cases.

The Privacy Act of 1974 (codified as 5 U.S.C. § 552a) is a foundational federal law that establishes a code of fair information practices for how federal agencies handle personal data.

Require Public Notice: This mandates that agencies publish a System of Records Notice (SORN) in the Federal Register for every database that retrieves information by a personal identifier.

8 U.S. Code § 1324 - Bringing in and harboring certain aliens is a federal criminal statute that primarily prohibits the smuggling, transporting, and harboring of unauthorized aliens. Legally referred to as "Bringing in and harboring certain aliens," it serves as a cornerstone for federal immigration enforcement.

Other important Cases:

In **Trezevant v. City of Tampa**, 741 F.2d 336 (11th Cir. 1984), the U.S. Court of Appeals for the Eleventh Circuit affirmed a $25,000 jury **award** for James C. Trezevant, who was unconstitutionally incarcerated for 23 minutes following a traffic stop.

Murdock v. Pennsylvania, 319 U.S. 105 (1943)
"The right to travel is a part of liberty of which **We the People** cannot be deprived without due process of the law under the 5th Amendment."

Shuttlesworth v. City of Birmingham, Alabama, 373 U.S, 262 (1963)
"There can be no sanction or penalty imposed upon one because of his exercise of Constitutional rights."

Sherar v. Cullen, 481 F. 2d 945 (9th Cir. 1973)
"The streets of a city belong to the people of the state, and the use thereof is an inalienable right of every citizen."

Brown v. Texas, 443 U.S. 47 (1979)
This landmark case established that police cannot force a person to identify themselves without reasonable suspicion that they are involved in a crime.

Schectman v. Dulles 96 Appellate DC 287, 225 F2d 938, at 941 (D.C. Cir. 1955)
"With regard particularly to the U.S. Constitution, it is elementary that a right secured or protected by that cannot be overthrown or impaired by any state police authority."

Canelsha Mills et al v. DC, No. 08-7127 (D.C. Cir. 2009)
"The right of the people to drive on the public street with freedom from police interference, unless he is engaged in suspicious conduct

associated in some manner with criminality, is a fundamental CONSTITUTIONAL RIGHT which must be protected by the courts."

In City of Indianapolis v. Edmond (2000)
"The U.S. Supreme Court ruled that police may not conduct vehicle checkpoints with the primary purpose of general crime control, such as drug interdiction. The Court held 6–3 that such suspicion less stops violate the Fourth Amendment because they lack individualized suspicion and do not serve a specific special need beyond ordinary law enforcement."

Garris v. Rowland, 678 F.2d 1264 (5th Cir. 1982), is a landmark United States Court of Appeals for the Fifth Circuit decision concerning Section 1983 civil rights claims and police liability for wrongful arrest.

The case involved **Walter E. Garris** who sued **G.F. Rowland** (an officer with the Fort Worth Police Department) and the City of Fort Worth. Garris alleged his constitutional rights were violated when he was arrested without probable cause for a crime he did not commit.

Hale v Hale, 201 US 43, 26 S.Ct.370, 50 L.Ed.652
"The innocent individual who is harmed by an abuse of government authority is assured that he will be compensated for his injury."

Hoffman v. United States, 341 U.S. 479 (1951)
In an 8-1 ruling, the Supreme Court established a broad protection for the privilege against self-incrimination under the Fifth Amendment. Samuel Hoffman was convicted of criminal contempt for refusing to answer questions before a federal grand jury. The Court held that the privilege extends not only to answers that would directly support a conviction, but also to those that furnish a link in

the chain of evidence needed for prosecution.

Norton v. Shelby County (1886) was a U.S. Supreme Court case about invalid county bonds, famous for the declaration that an unconstitutional act is as inoperative as though it had never been passed, establishing that de facto officers (acting under an unconstitutional law) have no legal authority. Justice Field wrote, "*An unconstitutional act is not a law; it confers no rights; it imposes no duties; it affords no protection; it creates no office; it is, in legal contemplation, as inoperative as though it had never been passed.*"

Gilmere v. City of Atlanta, 737 F.2d 894 (11th Cir. 1984), was a federal civil rights case addressing police brutality and municipal liability under 42 U.S.C. § 1983. The court held that police officers' fatal shooting of a citizen violated constitutional rights, and that the existence of state tort remedies did not prevent a federal § 1983 claim.

Thompson v. Smith, 155 Va. 367, 154 S.E. 579 (1930), is a landmark Supreme Court of Appeals of Virginia case often cited in discussions regarding the right to travel and the delegation of legislative power.

Right vs. Privilege: The court famously declared that the use of public highways for travel is a common right rather than a mere privilege. While this right is subject to reasonable police power regulation for public safety, it cannot be arbitrarily denied or prohibited.

Shapiro v. Thompson, 394 U.S. 618 (1969) remains a landmark case for its recognition of the right to travel as a fundamental right and for applying strict scrutiny to state laws that discriminate against new residents. This precedent was later reinforced in cases like Saenz v. Roe (1999), which also struck down tiered welfare benefit systems.

In Collins v. Virginia (2018), the U.S. Supreme Court ruled 8–1 that the Fourth Amendment's automobile exception does not permit a police officer to enter the **curtilage** of a home without a warrant to search a vehicle. The Court held that while officers can generally search mobile vehicles with only probable cause, they cannot bypass the constitutional protections afforded to a home and its immediate surrounding area (the curtilage) to access that vehicle. The automobile exception states is an exception to the general requirement of a warrant for searches and seizures under the Fourth Amendment.
https://www.law.cornell.edu/wex/automobile_exception

Lange v. California (2021), the U.S. Supreme Court ruled unanimously that the pursuit of a fleeing misdemeanor suspect does **not** automatically justify a warrantless entry into a home.
https://www.law.cornell.edu/search/searchResultsForm.html

Brendlin v. California (2007) is a landmark Supreme Court case establishing that passengers in a private vehicle are "seized" during a traffic stop, just like the driver. Consequently, passengers can challenge the constitutionality of a traffic stop under the Fourth Amendment and move to suppress evidence found during an unlawful stop. https://www.oyez.org/cases/2006/06-8120, https://www.law.cornell.edu/supct/cert/06-8120

Definitions

Bouvier's Law Dictionary, 1914, p. 2961
"**RIGHT** – A legal Right, a constitutional Right means a Right protected by the law, by the constitution, but the government does not create the idea of Right or original Right, it acknowledges them."

Due process of law is a constitutional guarantee (5th and 14th Amendments) ensuring that the government cannot deprive any person of life, liberty, or property without fair, established legal procedures. It mandates notice, an opportunity to be heard, and a fair hearing before an impartial tribunal. https://www.law.cornell.edu/
Addington v. Texas, 441 U.S. 418, 425 (1979) "The Due Process Clause applies to all 'persons' within the United States, including aliens, whether their presence here is lawful, unlawful, temporary, or permanent." Zadvydas, 533 U.S. at 693.

Probable cause is the legal standard, derived from the Fourth Amendment, requiring police to have sufficient, reasonable facts and evidence - more than a mere hunch but less than absolute certainty - to believe a crime has been committed or that evidence exists in a specific location before making arrests or conducting searches. If probable cause is not established, evidence obtained may be suppressed in court.

A Bill of Particulars is a formal, written legal document used in civil and criminal cases to demand that the opposing party provide more detailed, specific information about the general claims or allegations made in their complaint, petition, or indictment. It acts as an extension of the pleadings, narrowing the scope of the case to prevent surprises at trial and allowing the defendant to properly prepare their defense.

Legal standing, or locus standi, is the legal right or capacity of a party to bring a lawsuit or initiate legal proceedings in court. It ensures that only individuals or entities directly affected by a specific harm or dispute - rather than bystanders - can sue. To have standing, a party must demonstrate a sufficient connection to and harm from the action being challenged.

A Writ of Habeas Corpus under 28 U.S.C. § 2241 is a legal action used by individuals in federal custody to challenge the legality of their detention, including pre-trial detention, immigration detention, or execution of a sentence (e.g., calculation of time), rather than the conviction itself.
https://www.law.cornell.edu/uscode/text/28/2241

42 U.S.C. § 1983: The primary federal statute used by individuals to sue state or local officials for constitutional violations, including excessive force.

Use of Force - In the United States, use-of-force case law is primarily governed by the Fourth Amendment, which protects individuals from unreasonable seizures. Recent Supreme Court rulings have expanded the scope of what courts must consider when determining if an officer's actions were constitutional.

The Objective Reasonableness Standard

The foundational rule for all use-of-force cases comes from **Graham v. Connor (1989)**, which established that an officer's actions must be objectively reasonable.

- Perspective: Reasonableness must be judged from the perspective of a reasonable officer on the scene, rather than with the 20/20 vision of hindsight.

- The Graham Factors: To determine reasonableness, courts must look at the following items:

  1. the severity of the crime at issue
  2. whether the suspect poses an immediate threat to the safety of officers or others
  3. whether the suspect is actively resisting arrest or attempting to evade by flight
  4. **Tennessee v. Garner (1985) r**uled that deadly force may only be used to prevent escape if the officer has probable cause to believe the suspect poses a significant threat of death or serious physical injury to the officer or others.
  5. **Scott v. Harris (2007)** clarified that a police officer's attempt to terminate a high-speed car chase that threatens the lives of innocent bystanders does not violate the Fourth Amendment, even if it places the fleeing motorist at risk of serious injury.

Excessive use of force cases are primarily governed by the Fourth Amendment's objective reasonableness standard, as established in *Graham v. Connor* (1989), which evaluates if an officer's actions were reasonable based on the scene's circumstances rather than hindsight. Recent rulings, such as *Barnes v. Felix* (2025), emphasize considering the totality of circumstances, including actions leading up to the force.

Deadly force case law hinges on objective reasonableness under the Fourth Amendment, permitting lethal force when an officer reasonably believes a suspect poses an imminent threat of death or serious injury. Key rulings, notably *Graham v. Connor* (1989) and *Tennessee v. Garner* (1985), establish that force must be evaluated based on the totality of circumstances, not 20/20 hindsight.

Qualified Immunity is a legal doctrine created by the U.S. Supreme Court that protects state and local officials, including police officers, from individual liability in civil lawsuits. It shields government officials from being sued for actions performed within their duty, unless they violated a clearly established statutory or constitutional right.

Vi Coactus - The phrase means "constrained by force" or coerced, signifying that the signer did not provide free consent. It is sometimes marked as "V.C." alongside a signature, or historically**,** by adding an ellipsis (three dots) to indicate restricted freedom.

TDC – Threat, Duress, Coercion.

Bivens Actions allow individuals to sue federal agents for constitutional violations, but recent Supreme Court rulings, notably *Egbert v. Boule* (2022), have severely restricted its application. While used for excessive force or unlawful search, success is rare due to special factors counseling hesitation.

Article Links and Legislative Responses: As of early 2026, some states like *Illinois and New York* are proposing or enacting "State Bivens Acts" to provide local pathways for holding federal officers accountable.

- https://legiscan.com/IL/text/HB1312/id/3283065
- https://nysba.org/new-york-state-bar-association-supports-governor-hochuls-proposals-to-protect-new-yorkers-

constitutional-rights/

- https://lawecommons.luc.edu/cgi/viewcontent.cgi?article=1735&context=facpubs

- https://ag.ny.gov/police-departments-law-enforcement/immigration-enforcement

- NYC Mayor Mamdani signs landmark executive order limiting ICE access to NYC: https://www.trtworld.com/article/642737794b6b

- Qualified Immunity is a formidable barrier to most civil rights lawsuits, but the Federal Tort Claims Act is one potential remedy - https://www.ms.now/opinion/ice-lawsuit-qualified-immunity-civil-rights. https://share.google/W0pjCpPv7oyw3IxOk
- Judge Rebukes Masked ICE Arrests as 'Secret-Policing' Regime(1) - https://news.bloomberglaw.com/us-law-week/us-judge-rebukes-masked-ice-arrests-as-secret-policing-regime, https://www.wvsd.uscourts.gov/sites/wvsd/files/opinions/2_26-cv-00066_Goodwin2-19-26.pdf

The Federal Tort Claims Act (FTCA) of 1946 is a law that allows private citizens to sue the United States government for monetary damages for personal injury, death, or property damage caused by the negligent or wrongful acts of federal employees acting within the scope of their employment. It acts as a limited waiver of the government's sovereign immunity, making the U.S. liable similarly to a private individual under local laws. https://www.congress.gov/crs-product/R45732

- **Process:** Claims must be filed with the appropriate federal agency, usually via a Standard Form 95 (SF95), within two years of the incident. https://www.gas.gov/system/files/SF95-07a.pdf

The Freedom of Information Act (FOIA), 5 U.S.C. § 552, (1966) is a federal law that grants any person the right to request access to records and information from federal executive branch agencies. It promotes government transparency by requiring disclosure of documents unless they fall under nine specific exemptions, such as national security or personal privacy. https://foia.gov/faq.html

A Tort is a civil wrongdoing that causes harm or loss to another person, resulting in legal liability for the person who committed the act (tortfeasor). Unlike criminal law, which punishes acts against society, tort law focuses on compensating the victim and making them whole again, typically through monetary damages. Torts fall into three categories: Intentional torts, Negligent torts, and Strict liability torts. https://www.law.cornell.edu/wex/tort

In law, negligence is the failure to exercise the level of care that a reasonably prudent person would have used under similar circumstances. It is a foundational concept of tort law, focusing on accidental conduct or omissions that result in harm to others, rather than intentional acts. The four elements of negligence are: duty of care, breach of duty, causation, and damages. https://www.law.cornell.edu/wex/negligence

- **Types of Negligence:**
  - Ordinary Negligence: a standard failure to use reasonable care
  - Gross Negligence: an extreme departure from reasonable conduct, showing a reckless disregard for the safety or rights of others
  - Negligence Per Se when a defendant is automatically considered negligent because they violated a specific statute designed to protect the public (e.g., speeding in a school zone)
  - Comparative/Contributory Negligence: Legal doctrines used to determine if the plaintiff's own actions contributed to their injury, which may reduce or bar their financial recovery.

The primary difference between **Common Law** (also known as law of the land) and **Admiralty** Jurisdiction (also known as Maritime Jurisdiction) lies in the territory of the incident, the nature of the dispute, and the procedural rules used in court. See table below: https://www.fjc.gov/

Common Law Jurisdiction vs Admiralty / Maritime Jurisdiction:

Feature	Common Law Jurisdiction	Admiralty / Maritime Jurisdiction
Constitutional Basis	Rooted in state common law traditions; may arise under diversity jurisdiction in federal court	Article III of the U.S. Constitution extends judicial power to admiralty and maritime cases
Primary Location of Dispute	Land-based events or non-navigable waters	Navigable waters used for interstate or foreign commerce
Nature of Cases	Contracts, torts, property disputes, criminal matters	Maritime contracts, ship collisions, salvage, seamen's wages, marine insurance, prize cases
Type of Action	In personam (against a person or entity)	In personam and in rem (against a vessel or property itself)
Trial by Jury	Preserves right to jury trial	Typically no jury; judge decides
Standard of Fault	Often modified comparative negligence	Pure comparative negligence under maritime law
Procedural Rules	State rules or Federal Rules of Civil Procedure	Federal Rules with Supplemental Admiralty Rules
Exclusive vs Concurrent Jurisdiction	State courts primarily; federal courts via diversity or federal question	Federal district courts have original jurisdiction; Saving to Suitors allows limited state actions
Saving to Suitors Clause (1789)	Allows maritime plaintiffs to pursue common law remedies in state courts	Preserves concurrent state jurisdiction for certain maritime claims
Prize Cases / In Rem Proceedings	Not available under traditional common law	Exclusive to federal district courts
Historical Origin	English common law courts	English admiralty courts operating separately
Maritime Nexus Requirement	Not applicable	Must occur on navigable waters and relate to maritime activity

Footnote Citations

1. U.S. Const. art. III, § 2.
2. 28 U.S.C. § 1333
3. Judiciary Act of 1789 (Saving to Suitors Clause).
4. Federal Rules of Civil Procedure, Supplemental Rules for Admiralty or Maritime Claims.

U.S. Constitution Article III § 2

In all cases affecting ambassadors, other public ministers and consuls, and those in which a state shall be party, the Supreme Court shall have **original jurisdiction**. In all the other cases mentioned before, the Supreme Court shall have appellate jurisdiction, both as to law and fact, with such exceptions, and under such regulations as the Congress shall make.

The trial of all crimes, except in cases of impeachment, shall be by jury; and such trial shall be held in the state where the said crimes shall have been committed; but when not committed within any state, the trial shall be at such place or places as the Congress may by law have directed. https://www.law.cornell.edu/constitution/articleiii

Jurisdiction is the legal authority granted to a court or other official body to hear, decide, and enforce a case or legal matter.

- Without proper jurisdiction, any judgment rendered by a court is considered null and void. To legitimately decide a case, a court must typically possess both subject matter and personal jurisdiction. https://www.law.cornell.edu/wex/jurisdiction

Primary Types of Jurisdictions:

Legal systems use different categories of jurisdiction to determine which court is appropriate for a specific dispute:

- Subject Matter Jurisdiction: The authority to hear a specific *type* of claim. For example, a U.S. Bankruptcy Court has exclusive subject-matter jurisdiction over bankruptcy cases, meaning state courts cannot hear them.

- Personal Jurisdiction: The court's power over the *parties* involved in the case. This is often established if a person lives in the area, does business there, or has "minimum contacts" with the territory.
- Territorial Jurisdiction: The authority over events or property located within a specific geographic area.

- **Original vs. Appellate Jurisdiction**:
  - Original: The power to hear a case for the first time.
  - Appellate: The power to review and potentially reverse decisions made by lower courts.
- **Exclusive vs. Concurrent Jurisdiction**:
  - Exclusive: Only one specific court can hear the case.
  - Concurrent: Two or more courts have the authority to hear the same case simultaneously

https://www.law.cornell.edu/wex/original_jurisdiction

Webpage Links

The Constitution of the United States Explained:
https://constitution.congress.gov/
https://www.fjc.gov/

National Highway Traffic Safety Administration:
https://www.nhtsa.gov/
https://www.transportation.gov/
https://www.fmcsa.dot.gov/

ACLU: https://www.aclu.org/cases/morales-v-chadbourne
https://www.aclu.org/know-your-rights/stopped-by-police
https://shop.aclu.org/product/aclu-know-your-rights-book/aclu-kyr-book

Cornell Law School Legal Information Institute website link:
https://www.law.cornell.edu/
https://www.law.cornell.edu/wex/Standing

Institute for Justice: https://ij.org/

National Lawyers Guild: https://www.nlg.org/
https://law.justia.com/
https://www.quimbee.com/

UCC – Uniform Commercial Code:
https://www.law.cornell.edu/ucc
https://law.justia.com/codes/new-york/ucc/
https://www.nysenate.gov/legislation/laws/UCC
https://dos.ny.gov/ucc-forms
https://dos.ny.gov/uniform-commercial-code

UCC-1 Form: https://www.law.cornell.edu/wex/ucc-1_form
UCC - § 1-308. Performance or Acceptance Under Reservation of Rights:
https://www.law.cornell.edu/ucc/1/1-308
https://www.law.cornell.edu/ucc/1/1-207
Uniform Commercial Code (UCC) § 1-308 (formerly 1-207)
https://code.dccouncil.gov/us/dc/council/code/sections/28:1-308
https://www.oyez.org/
https://www.oyez.org/

Assaulting, resisting, or impeding certain officers or employees:
https://www.law.cornell.edu/uscode/text/18/111
https://www.law.cornell.edu/uscode/text/18/115
https://www.law.cornell.edu/uscode/text/18/1001

Code of Federal Regulations - § 390.5T Definitions – link:
https://www.ecfr.gov/current/title-49/section-390.5T
https://www.ecfr.gov/current/title-49/subtitle-B/chapter-III/subchapter-B/part-390/subpart-A/section-390.5T
https://www.law.cornell.edu/cfr/text/49/390.5T
https://www.law.cornell.edu/uscode/text/28/1291
https://www.law.cornell.edu/cfr/text/49/383.5

Google - Right to Travel:
https://share.google/aimode/c6oVfJXuRrEu48fEd
www.statenationalsrock.com
https://www.youtube.com/watch?v=WwgoBr3FJ7k

Bill of Exchange:
https://cirnow.com.au
https://www.law.cornell.edu/wex/bill_of_exchange

References

Some information obtained for this book came from either a Google search or from a YouTube video.

Books referenced:

- THE U.S. CONSTITUTION – Declaration of Independence, Bill of Rights, Amendments (Bonus: Fun Facts of the USA) Annotated: UNCLE SAM'S BOOK

- The Law Revolution, by Anelia Sutton – link: https://aneliasutton.com/
  Diplomatic Immunity Secrets – link: https://missionpossibleuniversity.com/

- HOW TO TRAVEL IN THE PRIVATE – A Lawful Guide of Freedom on the Roads - Written by: Steve Bardi, Kenneth Plaster, Ashley Rocks, & Gwendolyn Morris.

- I DON'T ANSWER QUESTIONS, Pleading the Fifth by David G. Ridings – www.NashvilleCriminalAttorney.com

- THE CIVILIAN RIGHTS HANDGUIDE – A CITIZEN'S GUIDE TO NAVIGATING POLICE ENCOUNTERS BY JOHN LANG

Final Note

This is not legal advice, but for entertainment and educational purposes only. If you can afford to, go to Staples or a neighborhood printer and create two signs - one for your vehicle and one for your home. Here are two examples.

<u>For your vehicle:</u>

I AM EXERCISING MY RIGHT TO REMAIN SILENT AND I WILL NOT ANSWER ANY QUESTIONS, AND I DO NOT CONSENT TO ANY SEARCHES. If needed, you can also state that you are exercising your 6th Amendment right to counsel. Always be polite in your answers and decline to answer any question(s) and never consent. Always ask: Am I free to go, or Am I being detained, if detainded plead the 5th and 6th Amendments and stay quiet.

<u>For your home:</u>

I DO NOT OPEN MY DOOR TO STRANGERS.

<u>TO LAW ENFORCEMENT OFFICERS</u>:

ENTRY REQUIRES A SIGNED VALID JUDICIAL WARRANT ISSUED BY A JUDGE. ADMININSTRATIVE WARRANTS DO NOT AUTHORIZE ENTRY.

THIS HOME IS PROTECTED UNDER THE:

1ST, 4TH, 5TH, 6TH & 14TH AMENDMENTS OF THE U.S. CONSTITUTION - THE SUPREME LAW OF THE LAND.

I DO NOT ANSWER ANY QUESTIONS, AND I DO NOT CONSENT TO ANY SEARCHES OR ENTRY WITHOUT A

VALID JUDICIAL WARRANT OR WITHOUT AN ATTORNEY.

COMMUNICATION: I RESPOND ONLY TO TEXT MESSAGES FROM KNOWN CONTACTS.

DO NOT KNOCK. DOCUMENTS MAY BE LEFT AT THE DOOR. THANK YOU.

Finally, if the United States Constitution cannot protect us from Federal Agents, then what kind of society are we living in and what does that say about the rule of law and **We the People**. I am fearful not only for myself, but for my neighbors, friends, family, and my fellow Americans. Shame on us. It is time for us to empower **We the People. They work for us. The U.S Constitution is the Supreme Law of the Land. No one is above the law; you cannot break the law to enforce the law.** I end with this from:

German Lutheran pastor Martin Niemöller (1892–1984)

"First they came for the socialists, and I did not speak out—because I was not a socialist.

Then they came for the trade unionists, and I did not speak out—because I was not a trade unionist.

Then they came for the Jews, and I did not speak out—because I was not a Jew.

Then they came for me—and there was no one left to speak for me."

Evil Prevails when Good People Do Nothing.

I want to thank the readers for purchasing this book, and I strongly recommend that you join a legal service such as LegalShield and learn about financial literacy. I have been a member of LegalShield since 2022. Here is my LegalShield link: ggideondunkley.legalshieldassociate.com, If you are interested in joining or learning more about LegalShield, click the link for more information.

Final Thoughts

Why Every Family and Business Should Have a LegalShield Plan:

- **The rich get richer because they hack life.**

  The rich get richer because they hack life knowing exactly how to protect themselves and make protective and profitable decisions because they get the advice of proper counsel first, so why shouldn't we? We now have access and there is no excuse not to protect and empower ourselves.

- **Access is no longer the issue - excuses are.**

  One of our most important expenses in business (and in life) is our legal cost to proactively use to avoid unnecessary torts against us. It's better to have it and not need it than to need it and not have it.

- **It's better to have it and not need it than to need it and not have it.**

  Legal emergencies don't schedule appointments. When the unexpected happens, the worst time to look for an attorney is *after* the damage is done.

- **Estate planning should not be a luxury - it should be a right.**

  Getting our Estate Planning done should not just be the privilege of the wealthy. It should be the right of every American. Anyone with family, business, real estate or social media needs one.

LegalShield makes estate planning accessible to everyone. Members receive a Will, Living Will, Health Care Proxy, and Power of Attorney—documents that most families never get simply because of cost or intimidation.

- **24/7 emergency legal access can change everything.**

  LegalShield provides immediate access to an attorney if you are questioned, detained, arrested, or if authorities attempt to remove your children from your custody. In critical moments, having an attorney *now* - not later - can make all the difference. This service has become a no-brainer in the society we live in today.

- **Real people. Real stories. Real lives protected.**

  There are countless success stories where LegalShield has diffused volatile situations, protected families, preserved rights, and in some cases, saved lives. I even have personal stories where I used the service with amazing results.

- **In the society we live in today, this service is a no-brainer.**

  Legal protection is no longer optional - it's essential! LegalShield's vision is to create Equal Access to Equal Justice for every American. We deserve and expect it, and if we don't know our rights we don't have any. The impact LegalShield has had on not only myself, but millions of those that reside in the United States is remarkable. I can't recommend it enough.

Thank you. God Bless you. Please stay safe, and may God Bless the United States of America, land that I love.
One nation under God indivisible with liberty and justice for all.

www.ingramcontent.com/pod-product-compliance
Lightning Source LLC
LaVergne TN
LVHW050922210926
848482LV00012B/508